Hello!

MW01131552

This book is perfect for children beginning to learn Chinese!

◊ Includes **30 Chinese words**.

◊ Features **large squares** for handwriting practice—Perfect for preschoolers.

◊ **Word formation** is included and the ability to **trace** each word.

◊ Includes engaging **illustrations in colour**.

◊ Includes the evolution of the Chinese words over time from **pictographs**.

◊ Plenty of **fun activities** such as dot-to-dot, a maze and spot the difference.

◊ Suitable for children learning **Traditional and Simplified Chinese**.

◊ We include the pronunciation of each word in two forms:

- **Jyutping**: A standard and commonly used phonetic system for spelling Cantonese using Roman letters (printed in orange next to each word).

- **Pinyin**: A standard phonetic system for writing Mandarin using Roman letters (printed in blue next to each word).

◊ This is aimed to be **cross curricular** and includes early maths activities.

◊ Perfect for **pre-schoolers** (3-5 years).

No prior knowledge is needed by the learner and there is no need for you to have any knowledge of the Chinese language either. The learner can view our **free tutorial** "My 1st Chinese Writing Workbook" on our website **www.superspeakjuniors.com**. In our tutorial we demonstrate how to pronounce each word in **Cantonese** and in **Mandarin**, as well as how to write them.

ISBN 978-1-8381799-5-3

One

jat1　　　yī

1

Two

ji6　　　èr

2

Three

saam1   sān

3

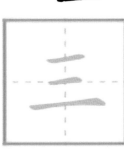 → 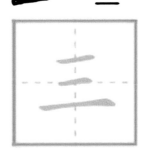 → 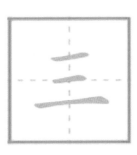 →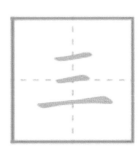

 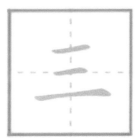 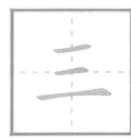 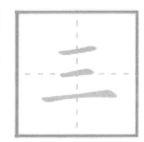

Four

sei3   sì

4

 → → →

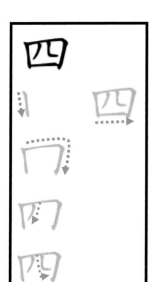

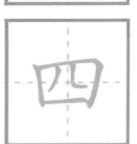  

All About Numbers

Match the numeral on the left to the Chinese word on the right.

How many things are there in each box? Count them in Chinese then write the number in Chinese.

五

Five

ng5　　　　wǔ

 →  →  →

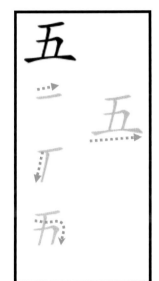

六

Six

luk6　　　　liù

 →  →

 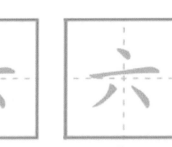  

Seven

7

Eight

baat3   bā

8

  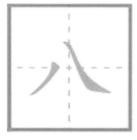  

 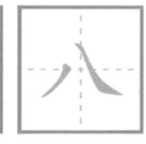 

Nine

九

gau2　　　jiŭ

9

Ten

十

sap6　　　shí

10

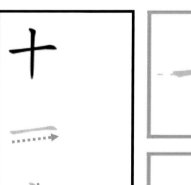

 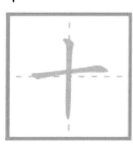  

 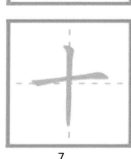  

7

Count The Sweets

Say all these numbers aloud in Chinese then write down how many sweets are in each row or draw the correct number of sweets to match the number.

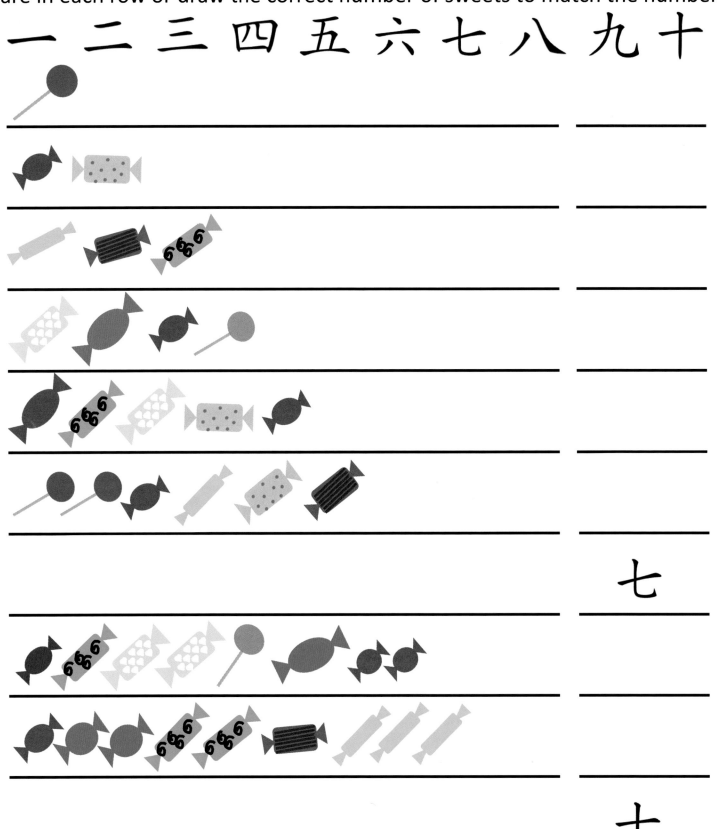

Dot-to-Dot

There are two dot-to-dot puzzles below. One has orange dots and one has black dots. Try to complete both of them then colour them in.

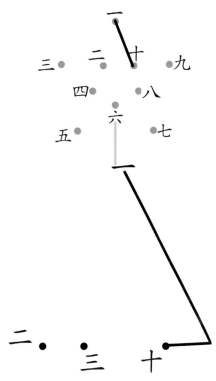

Person

人

jan4　　　rén

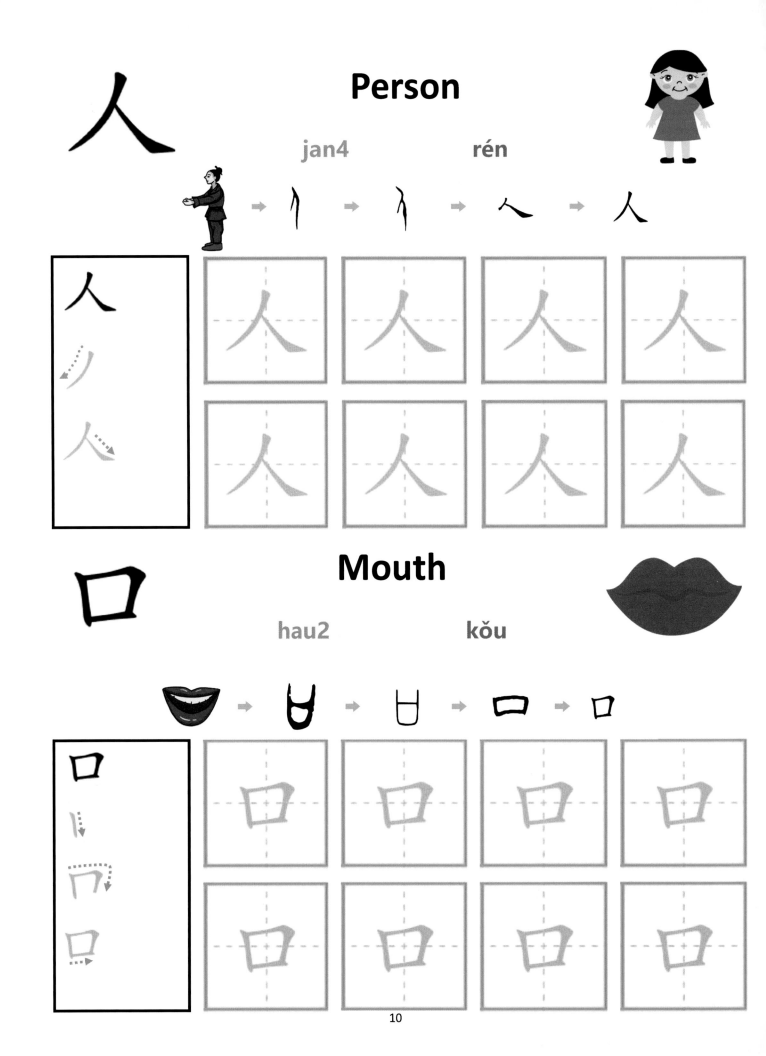

Mouth

口

hau2　　　kǒu

Big

daai6   dà

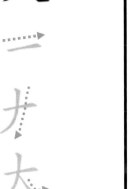

Little

siu2   xiǎo

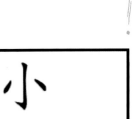

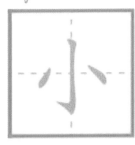   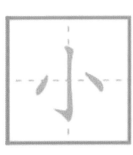

  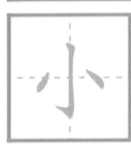 

Big Or Small?

Look at the Chinese word on the right and circle the picture that it matches. The first one has been done for you.

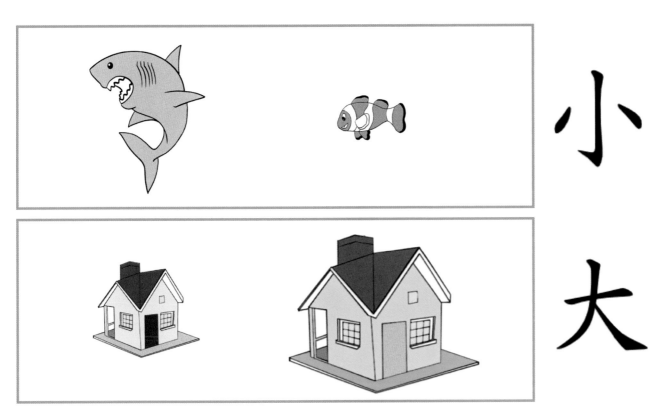

Match It

Draw a line matching the Chinese word to the correct picture.

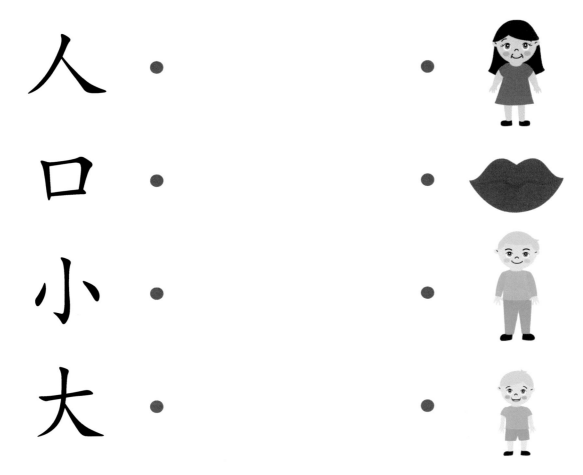

Soil

tou2   tǔ

 →  → 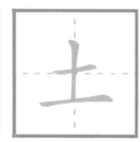 →  →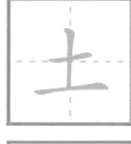

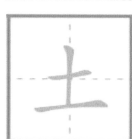  

Work

gung1   gōng

 → → 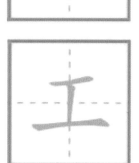 →  →

 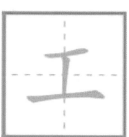 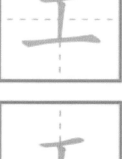 

Up

soeng6　　　shàng

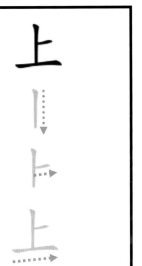

  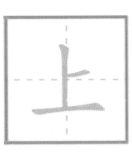 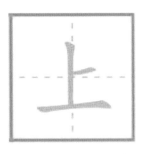

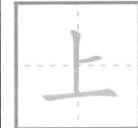  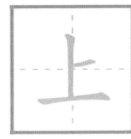 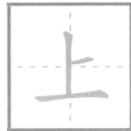

Down

haa6　　　xià

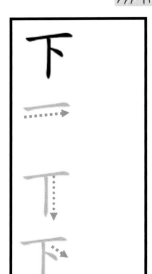

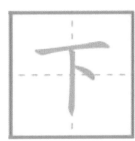   

Shapes

Count how many sides each shape has then write the number inside the shape in Chinese. Use the word bank below to help you.

一　　二　　三　　四　　五

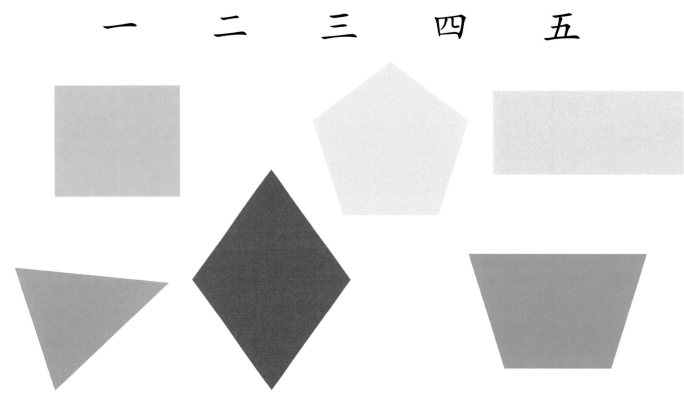

Missing Line

The words below are missing a line! Try to add in the line to complete the word.

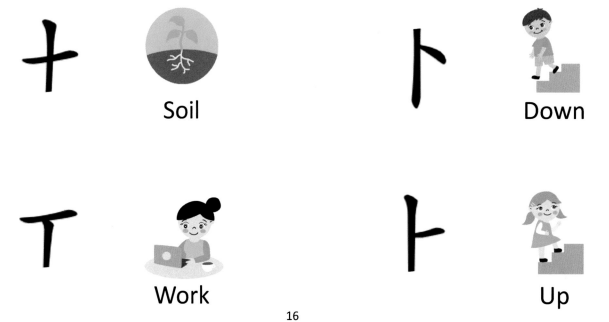

十　Soil

卜　Down

丁　Work

卜　Up

Mountain

山

saan1   shān

 →  → 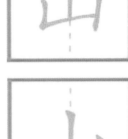 →  →

King

王

wong4   wáng

 → → → → →

17

Sky

天

tin1   tiān

 →  →  →  →

Water

水

seoi2   shuǐ

 → → → 水 → 水

18

Fire

fo2   huǒ

 →  → → → →

    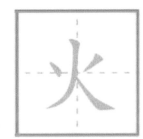

Wood

muk6   mù

 → → → →

Match It

Draw a line matching the Chinese word to the correct picture.

山　　•　　　　　　　•　

王　　•　　　　　　　•　

天　　•　　　　　　　•　

水　　•　　　　　　　•　

火　　•　　　　　　　•　

木　　•　　　　　　　•

Day

jat6　　　　　rì

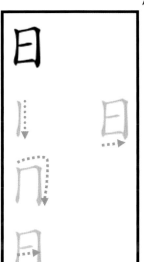

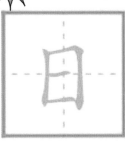 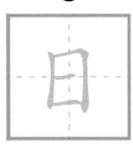 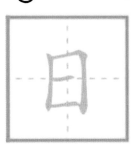 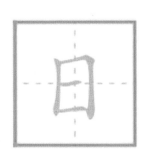

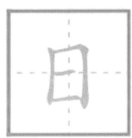 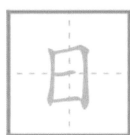 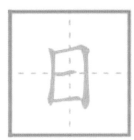 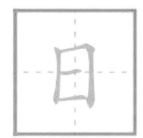

Moon (also means month)

jyut6　　　　　yuè

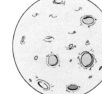

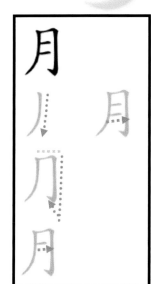

  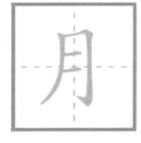 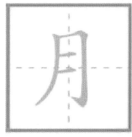

 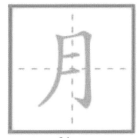 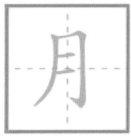 

Hand

sau2　　　　shǒu

 → → → →

Heart

sam1　　　　xīn

 → → →  →

Female

neoi5　　　　nǔ

 ➡ ➡  ➡ ➡ 女

Field

tin4　　　　tián

 ➡ ➡ ➡ 田 ➡

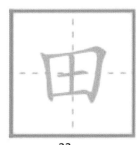

Match It

Draw a line matching the Chinese word to the correct picture.

日　　·　　　　　·

月　　·　　　　　·

手　　·　　　　　·

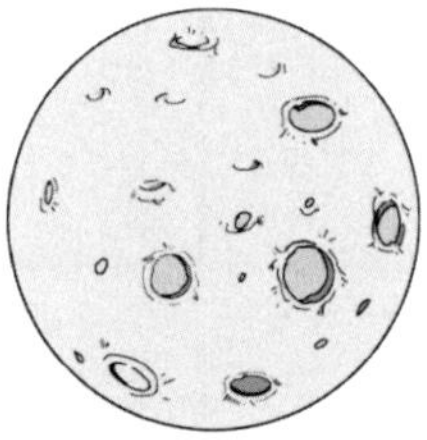

女　　·　　　　　·

心　　·　　　　　·

田　　·　　　　　·

Maze

Help Fred to find his friend John. Circle the Chinese words below if you pass them along your way.

田　　心　　木　　山　　火

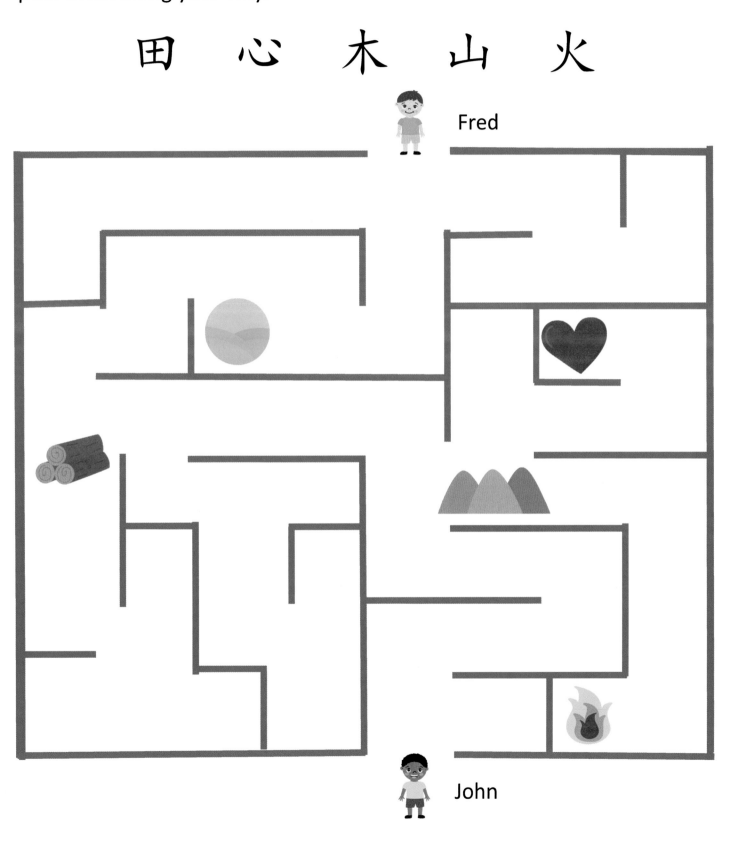

Number Ladder

Write the missing numbers in the spaces.

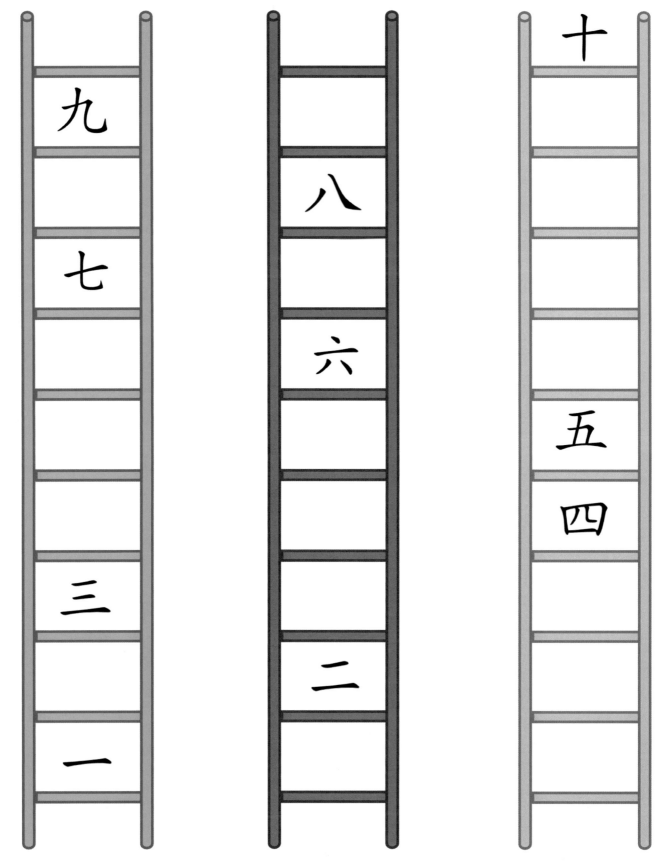

Addition

Add up how many items there are in each box then write the answer in Chinese.

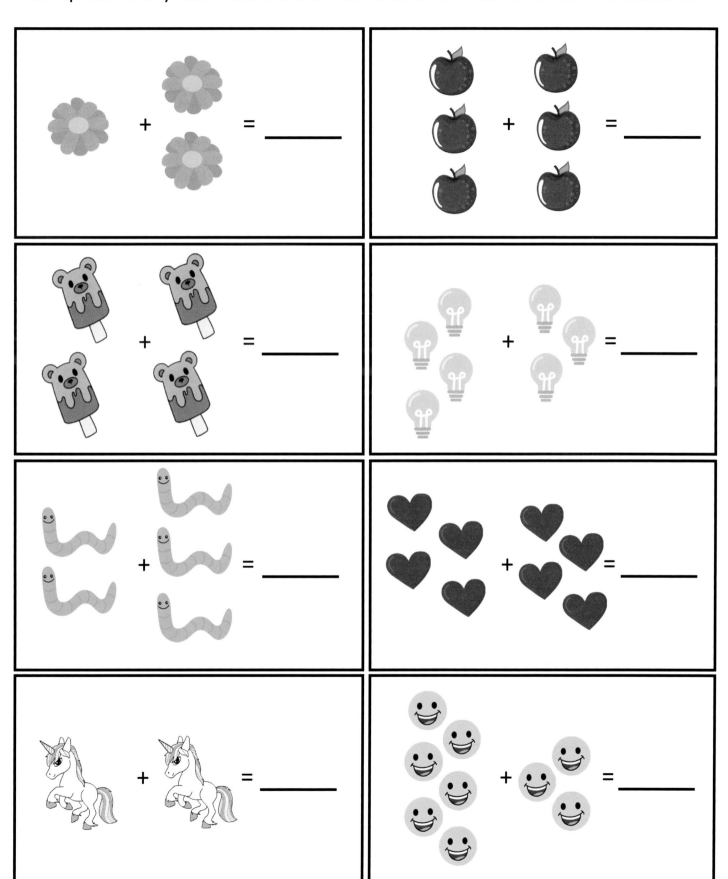

Spot the Items

Circle the Chinese words below if you see them in the picture. Not all the words are in the picture.

山　火　木　人　王

Spot The Difference

There are 5 differences between the two pictures. Can you spot them?

29

Colour

Colour in the numbers below.

Measure It

Using a ruler, measure the length of each vehicle and write the answer down in Chinese to the nearest centimetre.

_____ cm

_____ cm

_____ cm

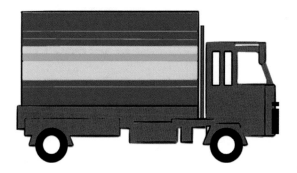

_____ cm

Which is Correct?

Look at the pairs of words below. Circle the correct words to match the pictures above them. The first one has been done for you.

四　口

一　二

土　工

日　田

人　大

水　木

上　下

手　天

火　大

水　山

小　心

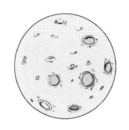

月　女

三　王

七　十

五　九

八　六

Chinese Zodiac Animals

In the Chinese lunar calendar, each year is named after an animal. Find your year of birth in the zodiac wheel to see which animal is your zodiac animal.

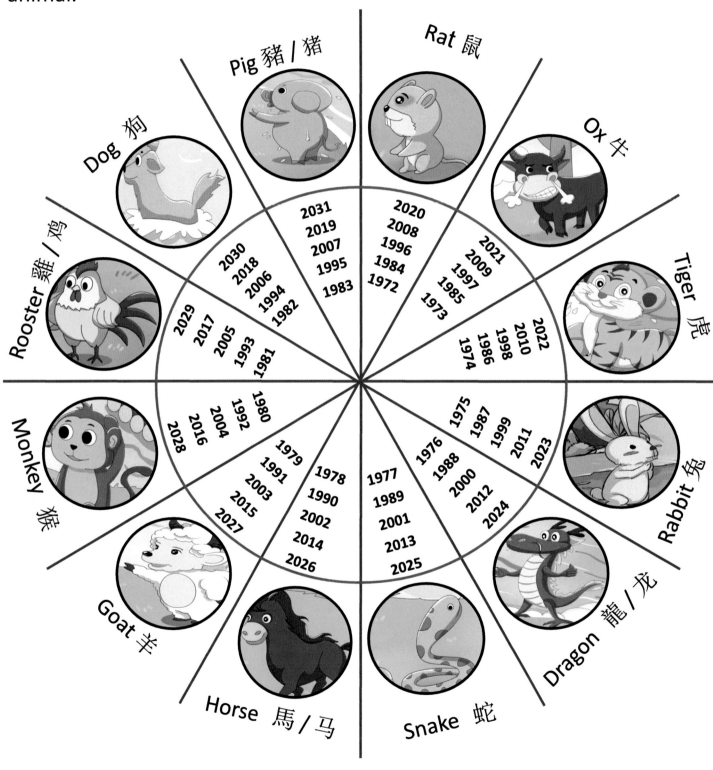

MY ZODIAC ANIMAL _____

Zhezhi Heart

Ask a grown-up to help you to cut out the red square below and fold it to make a heart. This is known as zhezhi in Chinese.

Certificate of Excellence

Congratulations!

_____ has successfully completed My 1st Chinese Writing Workbook.

Our Other Books

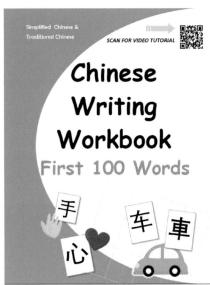

Chinese Writing Workbook

First 100 Words

Simplified & Traditional Chinese

with Pinyin & Jyutping

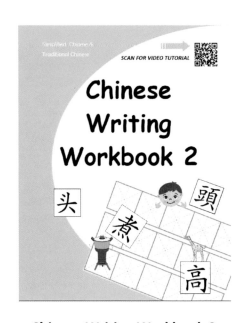

Chinese Writing Workbook 2

Simplified & Traditional Chinese

with Pinyin & Jyutping

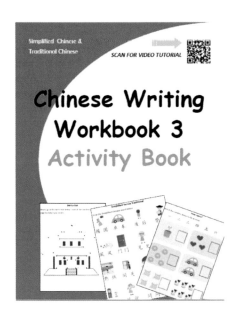

Chinese Writing Workbook 3

Simplified & Traditional Chinese

with Pinyin & Jyutping

Chinese Legends

Three Popular Stories

Bilingual Edition

English & Traditional Chinese

with Jyutping

Chinese Legends

Three Popular Stories

Bilingual Edition

English & Simplified Chinese

with Pinyin

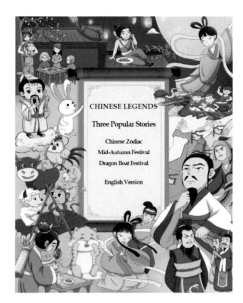

Chinese Legends

Three Popular Stories

English Edition

Answers

All About Numbers

Match the numeral on the left to the Chinese word on the right.

How many things are there in each box? Count them in Chinese then write the number in Chinese.

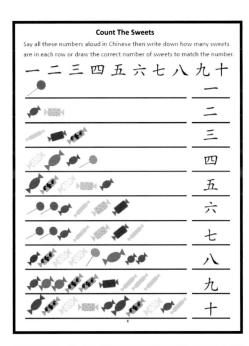

Count The Sweets

Say all these numbers aloud in Chinese then write down how many sweets are in each row or draw the correct number of sweets to match the number.

一 二 三 四 五 六 七 八 九 十

Dot-to-Dot

There are two dot-to-dot puzzles below. One has orange dots and one has black dots. Try to complete both of them then colour them in.

Big Or Small?

Look at the Chinese word on the right and circle the picture that it matches. The first one has been done for you.

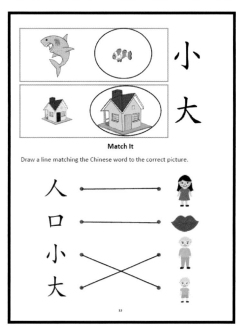

Match It

Draw a line matching the Chinese word to the correct picture.

人
口
小
大

39

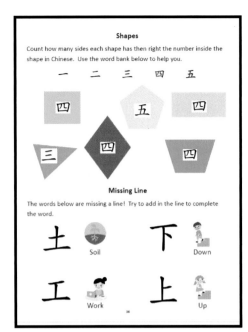

Shapes

Count how many sides each shape has then right the number inside the shape in Chinese. Use the word bank below to help you.

一　二　三　四　五

Missing Line

The words below are missing a line! Try to add in the line to complete the word.

土　Soil
下　Down
工　Work
上　Up

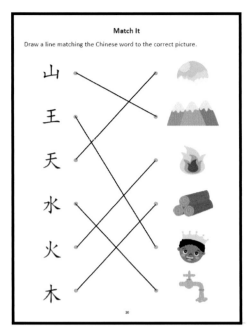

Match It

Draw a line matching the Chinese word to the correct picture.

山
王
天
水
火
木

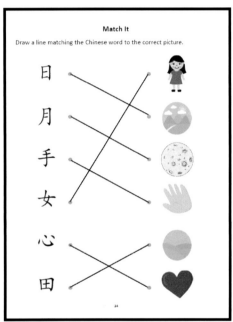

Match It

Draw a line matching the Chinese word to the correct picture.

日
月
手
女
心
田

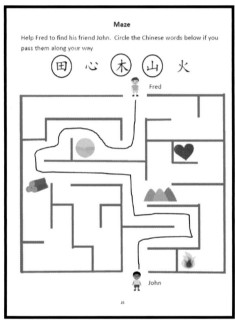

Maze

Help Fred to find his friend John. Circle the Chinese words below if you pass them along your way

田　心　木　山　火

Fred

John

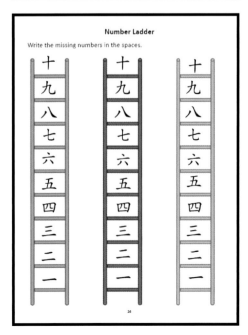

Number Ladder

Write the missing numbers in the spaces.

十	十	十
九	九	九
八	八	八
七	七	七
六	六	六
五	五	五
四	四	四
三	三	三
二	二	二
一	一	一

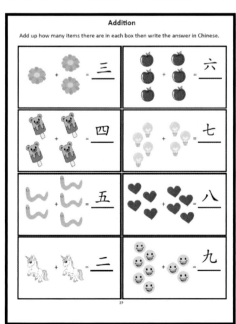

Addition

Add up how many items there are in each box then write the answer in Chinese.

三　六
四　七
五　八
二　九

Spot the Items

Circle the Chinese words below if you see them in the picture. Not all the words are in the picture.

Spot the difference

There are 5 differences between the two pictures. Can you spot them?

Measure It

Using a ruler, measure the length of each vehicle and write the answer down in Chinese to the nearest centimetre.

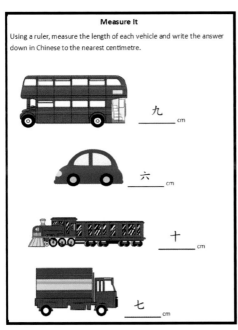

Which is Correct?

Look at the pairs of words below. Circle the correct words to match the pictures above them. The first one has been done for you.

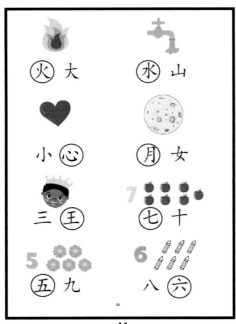

Manufactured by Amazon.ca
Bolton, ON